Body Image and the Media

by Celeste Conway

Content Consultant
Kim Walsh-Childers, PhD
Department of Journalism
University of Florida

CORE
LIBRARY

Published by ABDO Publishing Company, PO Box 398166, Minneapolis, MN 55439. Copyright © 2013 by Abdo Consulting Group, Inc. International copyrights reserved in all countries. No part of this book may be reproduced in any form without written permission from the publisher. The Core Library™ is a trademark and logo of ABDO Publishing Company.

Printed in the United States of America,
North Mankato, Minnesota
112012
012013
♻ THIS BOOK CONTAINS AT LEAST 10% RECYCLED MATERIALS.

Editor: Karen Latchana Kenney
Series Designer: Becky Daum

Cataloging-in-Publication Data
Conway, Celeste.
 Body image and the media / Celeste Conway.
   p. cm. -- (Hot topics in media)
Includes index.
ISBN 978-1-61783-782-1
1. Body image--Juvenile literature. 2. Self-acceptance--Juvenile literature.
3. Self-perception--Juvenile literature. I. Title.
155.9--dc14
                                    2012946378

Photo Credits: Maria Pavlova/iStockphoto, cover, 1; Marice Cohn Band/ Miami Herald/MCT/Getty Images, 4; iStockphoto, 6, 45; Evan Vucci/AP Images, 9; Monkey Business Images/Shutterstock Images, 10; Featureflash/ Shutterstock Images, 12; Shutterstock Images, 15; Morry Gash/AP Images, 17; Scott Gries/Getty Images, 20; Ron Galella, Ltd./WireImage/Getty Images, 23; Red Line Editorial, 25, 38; Ed Andrieski/AP Images, 26; Leanne Italie/AP Images, 31; Eugenio Savio/AP Images, 33; Sipa/AP Images, 34; Val Thoermer/Shutterstock Images, 36; Gareth Davies/Getty Images, 40

CONTENTS

CHAPTER ONE

An Ideal Beauty

One of the ways girls celebrate their birthdays is with a spa party. Girls as young as five and six years old have them. For parties at the popular Sweet and Sassy Spa, girls are picked up in a pink party limo. The birthday girl chooses from a list of different party themes. There's a Hollywood style party called "Night on the Red Carpet." At this party,

Four-year-old Gabrielle Egozi celebrated her birthday by getting a manicure and pedicure at Le Petite Spa in Michigan.

Teenage fashion and beauty magazines show thin and beautiful models.

girls get a movie star makeover. Then each girl gets a trophy at the Awards Ceremony.

Girls and boys are interested in beauty at a much younger age than ever before. Many say the media have influenced this change. The media include different forms of communication, such as radio, television, newspapers, magazines, and the Internet. Kids see pictures of beautiful celebrities and models everywhere. The girls are usually thin and pretty. The boys are tall with big muscles. These celebrities look perfect. Many kids admire them and want to be like them.

It's nice to be pretty. It's great to have strong muscles. Some kids, however, feel bad when they compare their own bodies to the perfect ones they see in the media. They may start dieting to lose weight. Some may try changing their looks in harmful ways.

What Is Body Image?

Body image is how someone thinks and feels about his or her physical self. It is an important part of self-esteem, which is how you feel about yourself. If you have high self-esteem, you feel really good about yourself. If you have low self-esteem, you probably do not feel good about your body or looks. Psychologists say that kids with high self-esteem feel better about their bodies than kids with low self-esteem. They do not judge themselves only on how they look. And they see their looks as just one part of who they are.

Kids who have a positive body image feel good about how they look. They do not think they are heavier or shorter than they really are. They like what they see when they look in the mirror, even if they do not look like models.

Kids who have a negative body image are not happy with how they look. Some of them can't clearly

First Lady Michelle Obama played soccer with kids as part of a Let's Move clinic.

see the size and appearance of their own body. They may see themselves as fat even when they are not. Having a negative body image can cause serious problems. Kids may become depressed. Some may try unhealthy diets. Others may use drugs, such as steroids or diet pills, to change their bodies.

The media are a big part of kids' lives.

The Media and Body Image

American kids spend approximately seven and a half hours a day using computers, television, video games, and other media. Many of these kids use more than one form of media at a time. Some researchers are very interested in how this constant use of media affects people. They wonder if media can influence how kids feel about their bodies. Most studies show that the media may have bad effects on young people's body image. Psychologists have studied how this happens. Most agree that it takes three steps.

1. People accept ideas about beauty that they see in the media.

2. They compare themselves to these ideas.

3. They try to change themselves to fit these ideas. Or they work very hard to keep a certain weight or look.

Body image is not a simple issue. The media have an effect, but family and friends also shape a person's body image.

EXPLORE ONLINE

The focus in Chapter One was the use of media and its effects on body image. It also touched upon the Let's Move program. The Web site below also focuses on the Let's Move program and childhood obesity. As you know, every source is different. How is the information given in the Web site different from the information in this chapter? What information is the same? How do the two sources present information differently? What can you learn from this Web site?

Let's Move: Learn the Facts
www.letsmove.gov/learn-facts/epidemic-childhood-obesity

CHAPTER TWO

Messages from the Media

In the United States kids watch between three and four hours of television a day. Throughout the day they view more than 3,000 advertisements. Often what the media present are unrealistic ideas about beauty.

Females in the Media

According to researchers from Westminster College in Salt Lake City, Utah, the beautiful girl on television, in

Angelina Jolie and Brad Pitt are a celebrity couple often shown in the media.

Thin = Good, Fat = Bad

In 2009 some Australian psychologists did an experiment. They showed pictures of seven different bodies to kids who were eight to ten years old. The psychologists asked the children to imagine what the people's personalities were like. The kids said the people with skinny bodies were happy, kind, and smart. They said the people with fat bodies were lazy, greedy, and not smart.

movies, and in magazines is often white with blond hair. She is tall and thin, weighing much less than the average female. Most models weigh approximately 23 percent less than women of healthy weight. Twenty-five years ago successful models weighed only 8 percent less than most women. According to the Girl Scouts of America Research Institute, nine out of ten girls say they feel a lot of pressure from the media to be thin. And 31 percent of the girls interviewed admitted to starving themselves as a way to lose weight.

Male models often have large and defined muscles.

Males in the Media

The media present ideas about how males should look too. Handsome men shown in the media are tall and have slim waists and hips. They are muscular, especially on their chests, arms, and shoulders.

Some boys who are underweight are ashamed of their bodies. They may start exercising excessively in hopes of bulking up muscle. They may spend all their spare time working out, neglecting school and friends. Exercise is not just a healthy, fun activity to them. These boys allow exercise to become the most important thing in their lives.

The Adonis Complex

In Greek mythology, there was a beautiful young man named Adonis. Goddesses fought over him because of his dazzling looks. Adonis knew that he was a prize. Some boys and men today want to look perfect. They think about their bodies most of the time. Psychologists call this the Adonis complex.

Steroid Use

Even boys who work out too much may think their muscles are not big enough. They may start taking powders and pills that promise to build muscle. Some kids even take steroids. These are drugs that help build muscle, but they can also be very harmful. Studies show that 5 percent of

DE NAME:

G.I. Joe action figures have very large muscles, broad shoulders, and thin waists.

school-age boys and 2 percent of girls use steroids at least once a week. Steroids are dangerous. They change people's moods and can cause extreme anger. Steroids slow down growth and cause acne and swelling in the body. Steroids can even lead to death.

Popular action toys for boys have become more muscular over the years too. Superman costumes for little kids now come with a puffed-up chest of muscles. These changes in toys show that even very young boys are getting the message that lean, muscular bodies are the best.

In a 2009 article for a medical journal, authors compared the body measurements of G.I. Joe action figures from different decades. They wrote:

> We purchased three [G.I. Joe] figures: a 1973 Adventurer with the original body in use since 1964, a 1975 Adventurer with the newer lifelike body, and a 1994 Hall of Fame figure. . . . Not only have the figures grown more muscular, but they have developed [more sharply defined muscles] through the years. . . . We also purchased several of the smaller [G.I. Joe] figures for comparison: a 1982 Grunt, a 1982 Cobra soldier (G.I. Joe's arch enemy), and a current G.I. Joe Extreme. . . . If [changed] to 70 [inches] in height, the G.I. Joe Extreme would sport larger biceps than any bodybuilder in history.

Source: Harrison G. Pope Jr., Robert Olivardia, Amanda Gruber, and John Borowiecki. "Evolving Ideals of Male Body Image as Seen through Action Toys." International Journal of Eating Disorders 26 (2009): 65–72. Web. Accessed July 12, 2012.

Changing Minds

This passage discusses the changes in the shapes of G.I. Joe action figures. Take a position on the changing body shapes, and then imagine that your best friend has the opposite opinion. Write a short essay trying to change your friend's mind. Make sure you explain your opinion and your reasons for it. Include facts and details that support your reasons.

CHAPTER THREE

The Impossible Goal

Looking like models and actors is hard to do. Looking good is a full-time job for them. And most have a team of people helping them to look their best. Their job is to project an image—whether it's in a movie or in a fashion magazine. Their image is what the media sell to their audiences. But this image is far from what the average person looks like.

Makeup and hair stylists get a model ready for a fashion show.

Tricks of the Trade

Most of the pictures in the media have been changed to make people look better than they really are. Digital artists can change pictures using image-editing programs on computers. Some tools they use include:

- Airbrushing: This makes a model's skin look perfect.
- Digital enhancement: This makes a model's hair look shinier or muscles look more defined.
- Photo manipulation: This makes a model look thinner. Even the shape of a face can be changed.

Scientists say that 95 percent of people do not have the kind of ideal body shown in the media. In fact, the media's ideal is becoming much harder for people to reach. This is because humans are getting bigger with every generation. They are also more overweight than ever before. A 2010 government study showed that one in three American children was overweight or obese.

Model Size

Yet models continue to get thinner. According to a story in *PLUS Models Magazine*, most runway models are so underweight that they are unhealthy. Many are

Cindy Crawford was a supermodel during the 1990s.

a size zero or less. Supermodels of 20 years ago, such as Cindy Crawford and Christy Brinkley, would now be considered plus-size models.

Television Shows

Some television shows are all about beauty, such as *America's Next Top Model* and *Extreme Makeover: Weight Loss Edition.* Even some television programs and movies for children are focused on beauty. There are many more thin characters in children's media than there used to be. In cartoons good characters are beautiful while bad characters are ugly. Some kids think this is true in real life.

Measuring Self-Image

One way psychologists determine how kids feel about their bodies is to use pictures. The pictures show different body types—from very skinny to very fat. The psychologists ask the kids to pick out the picture that looks most like their body. Next the psychologists ask them to pick out the picture of the body they like best. Sometimes there is a big difference between the two pictures.

Fashion Magazines

Many girls love fashion magazines. Eighty-three percent of girls read magazines for at least four hours a week. Many

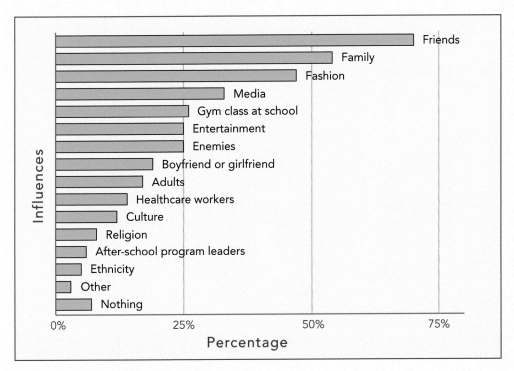

Influences on Body Image

This graph shows the results of a study by the Girl Scout Research Institute. It shows different influencing factors and the percentage of girls who believed the factors were a big influence on their body image. After reading about the study, what did you think was the biggest factor that influenced body image? How does seeing the study's results help you better understand what influences body image in girls?

of the articles in these magazines are about how to lose weight. A 2008 study by the Girl Scout Research Institute revealed that media, including magazines, and fashion were big influences on girls' body images. But friends and family were even bigger influences.

CHAPTER FOUR

Media's Effects

Media have different effects on their viewers. Ideas about the ideal beauty can come across in the media. But media can also be used to educate the public on healthy lifestyles.

Eating Disorders

Some think the media's focus on thinness is one of the reasons people develop eating disorders, such as anorexia and bulimia. People with anorexia have a fear

In 2007 Brittany Bethel battled anorexia, a disease that some link to how women are shown in the media.

of gaining weight. They eat so little they actually starve themselves. When they look in the mirror they do not see themselves as thin, though. Approximately 5 million to 10 million girls and women in the United States suffer from anorexia. Close to 1 million boys and men have anorexia too.

People with bulimia are also afraid of getting fat. They often eat large amounts of food. Then they make themselves throw up or use medicine to make them go to the bathroom. Most bulimics are girls, but 5 to 15 percent are boys. Some kids who have eating disorders have to go to special clinics to get help.

Online Bullying

Through online social media, kids can spread embarrassing or untrue information about one another. This includes opinions about how people look. According to Do Something, an organization for teens and social change, nearly 43 percent of teens have been the victims of online bullying. Nine out of ten middle school students were hurt in some way by online postings. And 75 percent of students had visited Web sites on which classmates were bullied. Online bullying can have lasting effects on a person's self-esteem.

Educating Viewers

The media can also be a great source of information. Many Web sites educate parents and kids about body image, nutrition, and healthy living. The Let's Move program Web site is a good example.

The media also provide forums where people can discuss issues. The popular *Dr. Oz Show*, for example, has dealt with topics such as body image, bullies, binge eating, and teen cosmetic surgery.

There are excellent films and documentaries about the problem of eating disorders, such as the PBS programs *Dying to Be Thin* and *Perfect Illusions.* Movies such as *Fast Food Nation* and *Super Size Me* have made people take a close look at the problem of obesity and junk food.

Some magazines are paying more attention to the issue of body image too. In 2012 *Seventeen* magazine responded to a petition from more than 84,000 readers who wanted to see more realistic images of girls on the magazine's pages. The editors of the magazine made a promise to show healthy models whose pictures have not been digitally changed.

Advertising Campaigns

Advertising can also be a powerful educational tool. Three models died of anorexia from late 2006 to early 2007. After Brazilian model Ana Carolina Reston died from anorexia in 2006, Italian fashion label

Julia Bluhm holds petitions to *Seventeen* magazine as she leads a protest outside the magazine's headquarters in New York in May 2012.

Nolita introduced an advertising campaign to bring awareness to eating disorders. People were shocked when they saw the billboards for this campaign. The billboards showed a skeleton-thin model who weighed only 68 pounds (31 kg). Italian fashion designers also banned size zero models from working in fashion shows.

The Campaign for Real Beauty was started in 2004 by Dove, a bath and beauty products company. The goal of the program was to get people to think in new ways about female beauty. Dove released the short film *Evolution of Beauty* as part of the campaign. It starts with a model who is not wearing makeup. In fast motion, the woman's hair and makeup are done. Then her photo is digitally changed. Her eyes are made bigger. Her face is made thinner and her neck longer. The film ends with the new image of the model on a billboard. She looks very different from how she looked at the beginning of the film. It shows the illusion of beauty that is presented by the media.

Body Mass Index

Body mass index (BMI) uses a person's height and weight to calculate how much body fat he or she has. To work in Italy, fashion models must now have a BMI of at least 18. That is still a much lower BMI than models and beauty contestants used to have. In the 1920s the winners of the Miss America contest had a BMI of approximately 22.

Brazilian model Ana Carolina Reston died from anorexia in 2006, sparking a protest in Italy against using models who are too thin in the fashion industry.

Isabelle Caro was the anorexic model used in the Nolita advertising campaign.

A *New York Times* article discussed *Seventeen* magazine's pledge to never change a girl's face or body in photographs. One reader shared with *Seventeen* how altered photos make her feel:

> Annette Okonofua, a woman who signed the petition, wrote: "I know that most of these girls on magazine covers are photoshopped, airbrushed and edited but yet, when you're looking at those photos physically, you can't help but think, 'Wow. I wish I looked like that.'"

Source: Christine Haughney. "Seventeen Magazine Vows to Show Girls as They Really Are." The New York Times. New York Times Company, July 3, 2012. Web. Accessed October 15, 2012.

What's the Big Idea?

Take a close look at Annette Okonofua's words. What is her main idea? What evidence is used to support her point? Come up with a few sentences showing how Okonofua uses two or three pieces of evidence to support her main point.

CHAPTER FIVE

A Positive Body Image

Many programs have helped educate kids and make them feel better about their bodies. The National Institutes of Health sponsored several programs on teens and body image. The results were published in 2008. They showed that for the teens in the programs the risk for developing eating disorders was reduced by 61 percent. The risk for obesity was reduced by

Body image is all about how you feel when you look at yourself in the mirror.

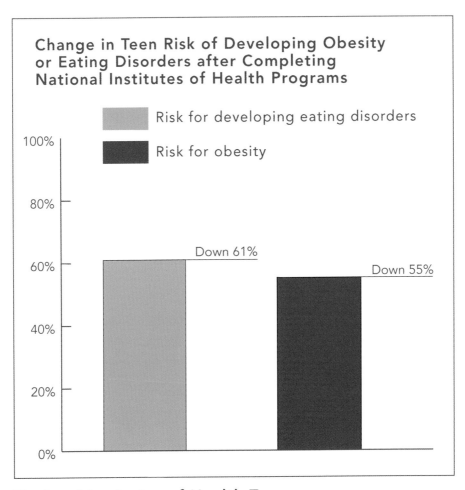

Change in Teen Risk of Developing Obesity or Eating Disorders after Completing National Institutes of Health Programs

Risk for developing eating disorders

Risk for obesity

Down 61%

Down 55%

National Institutes of Health Teens and Body Image Programs Results

This chart shows the results of the studies sponsored by the National Institutes of Health. Compare this chart with the text about the results of the studies. Does the chart help you better understand the results? How do the two sources present the information differently?

55 percent. Three years after completing the program, the teens still had positive attitudes about their bodies.

Healthy Body Image

Another program for elementary school kids is Healthy Body Image. It has shown good results. The program contains lessons with stories and activities. Students had more knowledge and felt better about their bodies after finishing the program. Kids are encouraged to accept and appreciate their sizes, shapes, and appearances. They also learn that it is natural for their bodies to change and sometimes gain weight as they grow. They are encouraged to eat healthy food, exercise, and avoid diets. The program also teaches kids how

Teen Truth Live

Teen Truth Live presents films and speakers for student assemblies. One of their programs is about body image and self-esteem. The presentation includes a 22-minute film with honest interviews of teens talking about their body image. It shows girls wanting to be skinnier and boys wanting to be more muscular. The presentation encourages teens to find their own real beauty, not the one shown in the media.

Self-esteem workshops, such as one put on by Dove in London, help kids think about their body image.

to tell which information in the media is true and reliable and which is not.

The media can be a great benefit to people. They provide instant news, information, and entertainment. It's hard to imagine life without media. Kids will continue to enjoy their favorite television shows, movies, and video games. It is also important to spend time with friends and family doing fun, physical activities. Not everything shown in the media is real though. Bodies come in all shapes and sizes. Understanding that helps people have a more positive body image.

FURTHER EVIDENCE

There is quite a bit of information about gaining a positive body image in Chapter Five. It covered programs that encourage positive body image in kids. It also discussed how media can educate viewers. What would you say was the main point of the chapter? What evidence was given to support that point? Visit the Web site below to see the *Evolution of Beauty* short film. Choose a scene from the film on the Web site that relates to this chapter. Does the scene support the author's main point? Does it make a new point? Write a few sentences explaining how the scene you found relates to this chapter.

Dove Evolution
www.youtube.com/watch?v=iYhCnOjf46U

IMPORTANT DATES

1920s

Miss America winner has a body mass index of 22.

1990s

Cindy Crawford and Christy Brinkley are supermodels in the United States.

2004

Dove launches its Campaign for Real Beauty.

2008

The National Institutes for Health publishes the results of several programs on teens and body image.

2009

A medical journal article shows that G.I. Joe action figures became more muscular from 1973 to 1994.

2009

Australian experiment shows that kids have good opinions about skinny people and bad opinions about fat people.

2006

Brazilian model Ana Carolina Reston dies from anorexia.

2008

A study by the Girl Scout Research Institute reveals that the media are one of the biggest influences on body image in girls.

2008

More than 160,000 kids have cosmetic surgery.

2010

The Let's Move Program is started by First Lady Michelle Obama.

2010

A government study finds that one in three American children is overweight.

2012

Seventeen magazine editors promise to show healthy models without digitally changed photos in the magazine.

Say What?

Studying about body image and the media can mean learning a lot of new vocabulary. Find five words in this book you've never seen or heard before. Use a dictionary to find out what they mean. Then write the meanings in your own words, and use each word in a new sentence.

Another View

There are many sources online and in your library about a positive body image and the media. Ask a librarian or other adult to help you find a reliable source on a positive body image and the media. Compare what you learn in this new source and what you have found out in this book. Then write a short essay comparing and contrasting the new source's view of body image and the media with the ideas in this book. How are they different? How are they similar? Why do you think they are different or similar?

Why Do I Care?

This book explains how body image is affected by the media. List two or three ways that the media affect your body image. Do you read fashion magazines? Do you compare yourself with actors and models in magazines?

Surprise Me

The way beauty is portrayed in the media can be interesting and surprising. What two or three facts about body image and the media did you find most surprising? Write a few sentences about each fact. Why did you find them surprising?

GLOSSARY

advertisement
information about something
someone wants to sell

anorexia
an emotional disorder that
causes a person to stop
eating because the person
has a poor body image

bulimia
an emotional disorder that
causes a person to eat too
much and then throw up
because the person has a
poor body image

cosmetic surgery
an operation to fix or change
a person's looks

disorder
a disease or other condition
that is not normal

influence
to affect someone
or something

muscular
having large and
defined muscles

obesity
a condition where one is very
fat or overweight

psychologist
an expert in the study of the
human mind and how
it works

self-esteem
a positive, respectful feeling
about oneself

steroid
a chemical that can
improve strength and
make muscles bigger

LEARN MORE

Books

Brashich, Audrey D. *All Made Up: A Girl's Guide to Seeing through Celebrity Hype and Celebrating Real Beauty.* New York: Walker, 2006.

Powell, Jillian. *Self-esteem.* North Mankato, MN: Smart Apple Media, 2006.

Trueit, Trudi Strain. *Eating Disorders.* New York: Franklin Watts, 2003.

Web Links

To learn more about body image and the media, visit ABDO Publishing Company online at **www.abdopublishing.com.** Web sites about body image and the media are featured on our Book Links page. These links are routinely monitored and updated to provide the most current information available. Visit **www.mycorelibrary.com** for free additional tools for teachers and students.

INDEX

ABOUT THE AUTHOR

Celeste Conway's books for young people span all age groups and include a picture book and several middle-grade and young adult novels. Conway lives in New York City and is an English professor at Berkeley College.